21st Century
Basic Skills
Library

HOW'S THE WEATHER IN THE WINTER?

by Rebecca Felix

Cherry Lake Publishing • Ann Arbor, Michigan

1

Published in the United States of America
by Cherry Lake Publishing
Ann Arbor, Michigan
www.cherrylakepublishing.com

Consultant: Marla Conn, ReadAbility, Inc.
Editorial direction and book production: Red Line Editorial

Photo Credits: Shutterstock Images, cover, 1, 12; Adrian Reynolds/
Shutterstock Images, 4; Aleksey Stemmer/Shutterstock Images, 6; Daniel
Cole/Hemera/Thinkstock, 8; Terric Delayn/Shutterstock Images, 10; ZouZou/
Shutterstock Images, 14; Jupiterimages/Photos.com/Getty Images/
Thinkstock, 16; Sylvie Bouchard/Shutterstock Images, 18; Mayovskyy
Andrew/Shutterstock Images, 20

Library of Congress Cataloging-in-Publication Data
Felix, Rebecca, 1984-
   How's the weather in winter? / by Rebecca Felix.
      pages cm -- (Let's look at winter)
   Includes index.
   Audience: 006.
   Audience: K-3.
   ISBN 978-1-63137-605-4 (hardcover) -- ISBN 978-1-63137-650-4 (pbk.)--
   ISBN 978-1-63137-695-5 (pdf ebook) -- ISBN 978-1-63137-740-2 (hosted
ebook)
   1. Winter--Juvenile literature. 2. Snow--Juvenile literature. 3. Weather--
Juvenile literature. I. Title. II. Series: Felix, Rebecca, 1984- Let's look at winter.

QB637.8.F44 2013
551.6--dc23

                              2014004488

Cherry Lake Publishing would like to acknowledge the work of The
Partnership for 21st Century Skills. Please visit www.p21.org for more
information.

Printed in the United States of America
Corporate Graphics Inc.
July 2014

TABLE OF CONTENTS

4

Cold

Winter is here. It gets cold.

The sun shines for less time each day. This makes it colder.

Winter

Sun

North

Earth

South

The northern part of Earth **tilts** away from the sun. The sun's **rays** hit it less **directly**. This makes it colder too.

Snow

Ice forms around dust **specks** in the sky. These become snowflakes.

Snowflakes fall. There are **snowstorms** in winter.

What Do You See?

What warm clothes do you see?

Changes

People **adapt** to the weather. They wear warm clothes.

What Do You See?

What kind of animal is this?

Some animals grow thicker fur to keep warm.

Frozen Ground

The ground gets cold in winter. Some plants die. Many stop growing.

What Do You See?

What is growing?

Soon, weather warms. Snow melts. Spring arrives.

Find Out More

BOOK

Raczka, Bob. *Snowy, Blowy Winter*. New York: AV2-Weigl, 2013.

WEB SITE

All About the Four Seasons—Easy Science for Kids
easyscienceforkids.com/all-about-the-four-seasons/
Learn about the weather during Earth's four seasons.

Glossary

adapt (uh-DAPT) to change to fit in a new situation

directly (duh-REKT-lee) straight from one point to another

rays (RAYZ) thin beams of light from the sun

snowstorms (SNOH-storms) winter storms where a lot of snow falls

specks (SPEKS) very tiny bits

tilts (TILTS) leans or tips to one side

Home and School Connection

Use this list of words from the book to help your child become a better reader. Word games and writing activities can help beginning readers reinforce literacy skills.

adapt	directly	less	snowstorms
animals	dust	melts	specks
arrives	Earth	northern	spring
away	fall	part	sun
become	forms	people	thicker
changes	frozen	plants	tilts
clothes	fur	rays	time
cold	ground	shines	warm
colder	grow	sky	wear
day	hit	snow	weather
die	ice	snowflakes	winter

What Do You See?

What Do You See? is a feature paired with select photos in this book. It encourages young readers to interact with visual images in order to build the ability to integrate content in various media formats.

You can help your child further evaluate photos in this book with additional activities. Look at the images in the book without the What Do You See? feature. Ask your child to describe one detail in each image, such as a food, activity, or setting.

Index

About the Author

Rebecca Felix is an editor and writer from Minnesota. Winters there are cold. There are many snowstorms. Businesses and schools there often close on very snowy days!